GROW

YOUR

POTENTIAL

ISBN 978-1-72-985540-9

FIRST EDITION (2019)

Printed in the USA

Published by Growing Potential

www.growing-potential.com

Grow Your Potential

A Teenager's Guide to Maximizing Your Life

Adam Norse

 **Growing** Potential

"This book is dedicated to my parents and family for always being supportive and believing in me. Thank you for teaching me that as humans, no matter your so-called standing in society, respecting each other and being nice is the most important thing"

Chapters

"Continuous effort — not strength or intelligence — is the key to unlocking our potential."

Sir Winston Churchill

INTRODUCTION

Do you realize that you are a unique masterpiece? You are a special edition. There's only one of you. No one can do what you can do the way that you do it. You have been put on this earth to do what only you can. You have greatness inside you. This greatness is a gift called potential. It is up to you to bring this potential to life.

This book contains practical advice and wisdom to help you start maximizing your potential. They are the things that I wished somebody had shared with me when I was a teenager. Instead I had to learn the hard way and waste a lot of time getting back on track, changing my thinking and un-doing bad habits. By no means are the tips and tools presented here all created by me — rather it is wisdom that has been around for centuries. I have just put it together in a way that I wished was available to me when I was in school.

My hope is that this guide will help you realize the unique gifts and talents already inside you, whilst also helping to prepare you for the inevitable challenges life brings. These chapters are by no means a definitive guide to guaranteed success; they are just a taster to set you on your way.

Take your time reading this book. Reflect on each chapter and ideally try to start applying the advice to life straight away. Go back to the book often. Carry it with you. Make notes and underline anything you feel you need to highlight. Most importantly, discuss new ideas or ways of thinking with your friends, parents, and family members.

Warning: fulfilling your potential is not easy. It is hard work. If you're not ready to give 100% effort, overcome challenges, break old habits and step out of your comfort zone then this book certainly isn't for you. Yes, it will be tough at times, but if you stick to it and stay committed then YOU CAN DO IT!

Maximizing your potential isn't a one-time thing or a destination. It's something that you do every day in all areas of your life. It's a mindset and a way of life. It's a lifelong journey of discovery and self-growth.

In the storybook of your life, you choose to be an extra or play the leading role. When you look back on your life, my hope is that you will be proud. I want you to live life to the fullest, pursue your dreams, and have a lot of fun along the way.

These pages are filled with advice, tips and practical exercises. I encourage you to apply them to your life and watch as you rise to your fullest potential.

GO FOR IT!

You've Got Potential

Potential lives inside all of us. It is a little seed of greatness, buried deep within you, that makes you unique. The word potential is exciting. It should fill you with boundless optimism and ideas of who and what you could become. Turning the seedling of your potential into a mighty oak tree takes effort, skill, sacrifice, and dedication. Unfortunately, most people give up before they ever see their potential begin to blossom. This is called "Unfulfilled Potential".

Unfulfilled potential is tough to deal with. It is heavy to carry around. It hurts to know that you're never going to become what you could have been. So much wasted opportunity. I will assume that because you are reading this book you want to learn how to maximize your potential. So, how do we set about doing that?

Maximizing your potential is easier said than done. It is by no means impossible, but it is hard work. You are going to have to commit yourself to growing across all the areas of your life. In order to grow you need to be fully engaged and dedicated. You must get to know yourself, and make honest observations about your attitude, mindset, and who you currently are. Eventually, you will begin to realize that you can't grow when you are always comfortable. You will get used to being uncomfortable — this is when you start to see yourself becoming the person you want to become.

Potential can either drive you forward or weigh you down. This all depends on whether you choose to dedicate yourself to developing it or you leave it on the shelf. The choice is always yours.

Hopefully you will choose to identify your potential and begin to apply the skills you read in this book so you can bring it to life.

"You will never know the power of your unique potential until you dedicate yourself to bringing it to life."

Define Your Own Success

Success is a by-product of maximized potential. If you focus on developing and making the most of your unique gifts and talents, you can consider yourself successful. Success and maximizing your potential go hand in hand.

Your own personal definition of success will determine if you are successful or not. Only you can determine the level of success you experience, nobody else can.

The world will try and force you to believe that success is having a mansion, a collection of sports cars, designer clothes, vacation homes across the world and, of course, a private jet. While that might be what success is for one person (that's ok if it is!), it certainly doesn't have be what success looks like for everyone else. Everyone's personal definition of success should be different.

The key word here is personal definition — not the media's definition, not your family's, not your friends' and certainly not social media's. That's why it is so important to have a clear understanding of what success will look and feel like for you.

For one person, success might be climbing the corporate ladder and becoming a CEO. For another it might be traveling the world and visiting as many countries as they can. Another might want to serve underprivileged communities in a developing country or raise a family. Whatever you want to do with your own life and whatever you want it to stand for — the decision is up to you. Nobody else.

"The definition of Success is always doing your best."

Just like potential, success is not a destination. Success is all about maximizing your own unique potential. It's about giving everything you've got and always doing your best. More importantly, it's about getting to the end of your life and having no regrets. This means following your own pathway on your journey through life.

I struggled with my own definition of success for many years. Not being clear on my own definition of success led me down many pathways which, with hindsight, were not the right ones for me. With this came a lot of confusion, uncertainty, stress, heartache and wasted time. Once I learned that I was the one who defined what success looked like for my life, I was able to move forward with clarity, purpose and focus.

Trust me, define what your own version of success looks like or, sooner or later, you're going to be unfulfilled and frustrated. If you don't define what success looks like for you, it'll be like wearing someone else's custom-tailored clothes. They fit the other person perfectly, but the measurements aren't quite yours. Wearing someone else's definition of success simply doesn't work, no matter how hard you try to squeeze into it.

Working out your own definition of success isn't easy. It takes work. But it is certainly worth it!

Take a blank sheet of paper or notebook. Ask yourself the following questions and write out the answers:

- Do you currently have a definition of success for yourself?
- Does anybody in your life already have a definition of success laid out for you? What is it?

- How does it feel when you think about following this path of success they've pre-planned for you?

- What are you good at?

- What are you passionate about?

- What would you do if you couldn't fail?

- When was the last time you got so caught up in something you were doing that you lost all sense of time? What were you doing?

- What would make you feel joyful, fulfilled and excited if you could do it every day?

- Now imagine yourself at the end of your life: How would you feel if you didn't get to pursue any of these things?

- What is YOUR personal definition of success?

Hopefully these questions will help you arrive at your own definition of success. Keep your answers in a safe place so you can reflect on them often. Know that your definition of success will most likely change as you get older and have more experiences. This isn't you being flakey or changing your mind, it's simply you evolving. As you learn new things about yourself, you can refine your definition.

You have the capability to determine whether your life is successful or not. Regardless of where life takes you, or the circumstances you encounter, if you commit to always doing your best every single day, then you will undoubtedly be a success.

"Only you decide what success looks like for you. Nobody else."

3

Mirror, Mirror on the Wall

When using a map, before you can start to work out how you're going to get somewhere you need to find out exactly where you are located. This is the starting point of your journey. You need to do exactly the same thing when looking to grow your potential. You have to work out exactly where you are on your journey so you can start to map out the route you need to take.

We call this self-reflection. It sounds easy in theory, yet in reality it is much harder. You will have to pause and evaluate your strengths, areas of improvement, attitude, and choices, and this can be uncomfortable. Many people don't want to have an honest conversation with themselves because they are afraid of what they will discover, or they are just too lazy. Ignorance is bliss. They don't have to get out their comfort zone to address anything, they can just continue freewheeling through life.

In order to maximize your potential, you cannot avoid self-reflection. It gives you your starting point. **The secret is to realize that there is no shame or embarrassment in what you uncover during these honest conversations.** Nobody is going to laugh at you or make fun of choices you have or have not made. In fact, you do not need to share your feedback with anyone else (although I do recommend finding a trusted friend so you can encourage and motivate each other).

"Self-reflection is simply having an honest conversation with yourself."

Doing self-reflection takes a lot of courage. You need to be brave. Most people don't want to do it, but you aren't most people.

Self-reflection exercises (see example below) are very powerful tools. You will get used to doing them and will be able to use them as you continue on the path to realizing your potential. These will help you identify your strengths, things you enjoy, and also areas that could use some improvement. Identifying specific areas where you need to grow allows you to focus on turning them into strengths. Although this is not an exact formula, I can say that the more honest you are with your answers, the more valuable insight you will have, which will make it easier to decide what you need to do to move forward in an area.

Below is a list of example questions to get you started on your self-reflection journey. As you grow and start to see some momentum you might want to create your own questions. The better the question, the more insightful and useful your answer will be:

1. What excites me most about the future?

2. What scares me most about the future?

3. How would my perfect day look? Be specific.

4. What do I want my life to stand for?

5. What am I doing about the things that matter most in my life?

6. Am I using all my gifts & talents?

7. Have I done anything lately worth remembering?

8. Have I made someone smile today?

9. What have I given up on?

10. When did I last push the boundaries of my comfort zone?

11. What one piece of advice would you give your younger self?

12. Who do I admire the most? Why do I admire them?

13. What do I need to change about myself?

14. How would my friends describe me?

15. Who has had the greatest impact on my life?

16. What do I want most in life?

17. What one thing would I like to achieve in life above everything else?

18. Which is worse: failing or never trying?

19. What's the one thing I'd like others to remember about me at the end of my life?

20. Does it really matter what others think about me?

"**Reflect** on your life often. People who don't should not be surprised when they find themselves at an unwanted **destination**."

Dreams Versus Goals

All of us have dreams inside that we long to come true. Dreams are exciting. They are filled with hope, and give us a taste of what the future might hold. Without the possibility to dream, life would often seem boring and overwhelming.

As much as dreams are inspiring and exciting, they can also be the exact opposite. Dreams that remain unfulfilled or even unattempted can leave us feeling full of regret, especially as we get older. In her book The Top Five Regrets of the Dying, Bronnie Ware wrote about her experience of working with sick people who were approaching the end of their lives. She said the most common regret as they looked back on their lives was that they didn't pursue their dreams.

To avoid getting to the final stages of your life and being packed full of regrets and "could have beens", you have to take action. **Otherwise, your dreams will remain just that: dreams.**

Let me introduce you to goals. Goals are the things that make dreams become a reality. By setting goals, you start to breakdown your dream into bitesize, achievable chunks. Slowly you begin to move towards your dreams, even if the idea of actually achieving it still seems a long way away or a distant possibility.

A goal is simply a dream with a deadline. For example, if you have always dreamed of running a marathon but can't find the energy to run around the block, a goal might be to run two miles by a certain date in the near future. Once you begin moving towards your target achievement, you will be filled with hope, and you will be one step closer to accomplishing your dream. Set goals that are both achievable and challenging, and you will keep inching forwards.

The key thing here is to dream big, but plot out your path to achieving your dream with goals that have a specific time frame. If you start to do this, you will soon see just how quickly you progress towards your dreams.

The most important thing on this journey is who you will become as your venture ahead in pursuit of your dreams. You will develop vital life skills like persistence, focus, effort, time management and mental toughness (to name a few) — these will provide a platform for your continued success.

So, if you want to make your dreams come true, or at least have a go at it, break your dreams down into goals. Otherwise, you might start to see them turn into nightmares.

"**Goals** are the stepping stones to achieving your dreams. Thinking your **dreams** will just come true without effort, sacrifice, dedication, and focus is nothing but **fantasy**."

Dream Big

All of us have dreams — so why not dream big? Everyone's dreams are unique, and they all mean something special to us. No dream is too silly or insignificant. It's personal to you. Your dreams make you YOU. You might have one dream, or you may have a few. Either way, don't be fooled into thinking that dreams are the stuff of fairy tales or just for children. No, your dreams are important and are special to you. And no one's dreams are bigger or more important than anyone else's.

Cherish and take care of your dreams. Guard them with everything you've got. Only share your dreams with people you trust and those who are going to breathe life into them. Avoid sharing them with negative or jealous people. Learn to protect them. Write them down in a notebook or journal. Putting them on paper is a major step towards making dreams become a reality. In doing so, you give your dreams life. Carry your dreams around with you. Read them often and don't lose sight of them.

Action and patience are two central ingredients for making dreams come true. Things don't just happen, you need to take the first step(s). Take action. Make a move. Things don't just happen instantaneously.

Dreams are a result of hard work, consistency, faith and patience.

For those of you who are sat there saying you don't have a dream — that is simply not true. All of us have dreams inside of us. Sometimes they come more easily to mind for some than to others. If you're having trouble, don't be discouraged. Spend some time alone with a blank sheet of paper and start writing down all the things you love to do. Think about what you'd do if you had a magic wish. Think the impossible!

"You need a dream, or else how will it ever come true?"

Write down at least one thing you love to do:

Write down one thing you would do if you couldn't fail (aka dreams!):

Read your dreams every day. Stop and reflect on whether you are moving towards or further away from them. Keep making progress. One step at a time. Day after day. Week after week.

Our dreams are not inside us by accident. They are there to be chased and lived out. It's up to you to make them a reality!

A key thing to realize is that as you grow, change, and develop as a person, so too will your dreams. It is okay if your dreams change, or what you desire is now different from what you dreamed about five years ago. This is to be expected. It doesn't mean that original dreams weren't real to you, it just shows that you are growing as a human and your dreams are becoming more finely tuned at the same time. Dream on.

"Chase after your dreams, no matter how crazy they seem."

Habits

You can be dedicated, focused, hardworking, and committed to realizing your true potential, but you cannot achieve it with bad habits. Here is a cold hard fact: if you don't master your habits, you will be left frustrated by your lack of progress.

Your life does not transform by changing a single thing. It comes down to a lot of little, daily changes, like changing bad habits or making new good ones.

As I have grown older and studied the lives of successful people, I've seen that habits are the one thing that sets them apart. Their habits help them to leverage and make the most of their skills and talents. By the time I got serious about maximizing my own potential in my mid-twenties (which is still a work in progress by the way!), I had already acquired lots of habits that weren't supporting me in being the best I could be. I had to rewire my thinking, actions and approach to many areas of my life. It was a long, sometimes painful process. It is much easier for you as a teenager to get into positive, smart habits in place now so you can avoid all the challenges that unlearning bad habits involves.

Whatever you want to do or achieve, whatever success looks like for you, habits are the things that will get you there. Habits control how we think, feel and act. Either you can decide to master your habits, or your habits will master you.

A habit is something that you do consistently. It can also be how you think, or your belief system. Before long, we have done this action or thinking so often that we don't have to think about what we are doing anymore. It becomes subconscious — a habit is formed.

Research by Phillippa Lally (2010) at University College London shows that a habit takes 66 days to form. This means we need to do something intentionally for 9.4 weeks before it becomes something we do without thinking.

Your challenge is to identify your current habits and determine whether they are moving you in the direction you want to go, or if they are holding you back. If you have positive habits, can you build on these? On the other hand, if you have negative habits you are going to need to rewire your brain and replace them with positive ones.

Achieving your goals and dreams and maximizing your potential hinges on your daily habits. They are the things that will determine your success or lack thereof.

The beauty of habits is that once you have mastered them you do them automatically. Since you don't have to think about them anymore, you free up more mental space for other, more important aspects of your life. The more positive habits you can stack on top of each other, the quicker you will start to build momentum in your life and begin to experience success.

"If you can **master** your habits, you have the **power** to **succeed**. If your **habits** master you, then be prepared to fall short."

7

Whatever You Choose to Be, Be a Good One

Everyone has their own unique gifts and talents. Whether you choose to a be a teacher, gardener, doctor, lawyer, gymnast, butterfly trainer, street cleaner, entrepreneur, chef, librarian, city worker...make it your mission to be a good one. Give it your all. Dedicate yourself to what you do.

Have high levels of excellence. Lead by example. Giving your all and maximizing your potential will bring you so much satisfaction and peace that other people will want what you have. Give it a try. I dare you.

"Do your **best** every day, in everything you **do**."

8

Create an Exciting Vision for Your Life

Have you ever tried to go somewhere without having a map or directions? More often than not, you end up getting hopelessly lost. I know that is almost always certainly the case for me.

Most people's lack of success comes from not having a plan for their life. You wouldn't start to build a house without an architectural plan, so why would you not do this when building your life?

This is your life, not your parents. Not your friends. Be wary of taking advice from people close to you who feel they know what is best for your life and what you should be doing. With the greatest love and respect, they don't know. Of course, they may have advice, experiences, ideas, and insights as to what you might do with your life, and you should definitely utilize their wisdom; however, please know that you do not have to follow a pathway or career that you don't want.

Culturally I know that families from some ethnic backgrounds put a lot of pressure on children to pursue a certain career path. Often the student doesn't get a say in the matter and they are just expected to obey the family's wishes. Whilst I am a big believer in respecting your family, I am more passionate about individuals maximizing their own potential – something that is impossible if your future is being decided for you. If this is you I encourage you to be brave and share your feelings with your family. I know this can often be hard and uncomfortable; however, in most cases, parents only want the best for their child and if they realize the pain they are causing they will listen to their desires. The worst thing you can say is nothing.

Having people close to you giving you guidance is priceless. It often comes from them loving you and only wanting the best for your future — but only you know what you want to do with your life. We know what is best for ourselves.

"Don't **settle** for somebody else's plan for your life. If you do, prepare yourself for **disappointment**."

Only you know what you're passionate about deep inside. Don't just pursue something because your friends are doing it and you feel you need to be seen doing it yourself. I have met too many people who have listened to people close to them when making life and career decisions that ultimately led them to pursue something that they hated.

Working out a plan for your life is not easy. There is no magic formula. It takes a lot of thinking, exploring and reflecting — it is hard and messy. It can take more than a few attempts to know what you really want to do. This is why most people don't do it. But you are not most people. You are different. You are on the path to maximizing your potential. Be bold. Be brave.

Spend some time planning what you want to do with your life. Don't worry you don't need to know your plan in exact detail. Just focus on working out your next steps. As you start to work out your plan, your pathway will begin to get clearer. Simply getting started is your first challenge.

9

Stop Comparing Yourself

As humans we begin to compare ourselves to others at a very early age. You'll even find children in elementary school comparing themselves to their classmates over topics ranging from the contents of their lunchbox, number of friends, test scores to bottle flipping. Comparing yourself to others is very natural. However, if you are going to maximize your potential, you need to fight against the black hole of comparison. Which is easier said than done.

The older you get, the more things there are to compare yourself against; house sizes, schools you attend, career or lack thereof, bank balance, the car you drive, number of vacations per year. You name it.

Simply put, comparing yourself to everyone else is a slippery slope to never-ending disappointment. It is a path full of dangerous potholes, littered with frustration.

Throughout your life you are going to be meeting new people wherever you go. If you are constantly comparing yourself and your life to everyone you meet, firstly, I can tell you that it's going to get tiring. Secondly, you are going to either become bitter and jealous, or you are going to become arrogant, thinking you are better than other people. Neither of these are fun ways to live.

"Always be a first-rate version of **yourself, not** a second-rate version of **someone else**."

You need to be comfortable in your own skin in order to avoid comparing yourself. You must celebrate your own individuality, and embrace that there is nobody else like you in the world. Your journey through life is unique to you. As we discussed in previous chapters, constructing your **own definition of success** is going to help you in carving out your own path, and will help you avoid sizing yourself up against everyone else along the way. **If you didn't do this in Chapter 2, go back and do it now.**

Everyone has their own gifts and talents to bring to the world. All our lives are going to look different, and they should. Imagine how boring of a world it would be if everyone was the same.

Comparisons are most always based on surface level things (cars, house, bank balance) and our own perceptions of other people's lives and what they have or do (job, status, background). What we can't measure through surface level things is how happy, joyful, fulfilled, or content other people are. We can't peer under the hood and see exactly what is going on in someone's life. Don't be fooled into thinking that external success equals internal success (or happiness). Tragically newspapers are full of stories about billionaires who are depressed, or music stars who take their own lives. Despite these people apparently having 'dream jobs' they still aren't fulfilled or happy inside.

Rather than compare and contrast our lives with what others seem to have or don't have, I encourage you to run your own race in life. Define what success looks like for you, construct a plan for your life, pursue your goals and dreams, maximize your potential — if you do all these things then, regardless of the outcome or the material goods you acquire along the way, you are a success. The only comparison you should be making is between yourself and all you have the potential to be.

"Run your own race. Remember that every individual is unique with their own special talents."

10

Do What You Love

Each of us have our own unique interests, likes, and dislikes. We each get excited and passionate about different things. When you're exploring jobs and careers, make sure you are looking at opportunities that interest you, things that you genuinely have a passion for.

Now let's be clear, I'm not talking about dreams jobs like a movie star or a chief taster in a chocolate factory. If you can get a dream job, that's amazing. It is important that we be a little more open-minded. That is not to say that if you don't manage to secure your dream job, then you have to give up on securing a job you like. Not at all.

When you are considering future jobs, look for something you are actually going to like. It is important to go for something you will enjoy. If you are an outdoorsy type of person, then a desk job sat behind a computer screen all day might not be the best match for you. Or, if you don't particularly like children, then being a teacher perhaps isn't the best role for you. Same with a zoo keeper — probably not a good choice if you are scared of lions.

Know that as you acquire more experience and skills, you will begin to learn more specifically what you like and don't like about your job. This will allow you to specialize further in a field and concentrate on doing more of what you love. Often we don't know that we will like, or dislike, in a job until we actually start to do it and learn exactly what it entails. It is a little like panning for gold — it takes patience and staying the course. Don't give up exploring and searching for your sweet spot. If you keep looking and remain patient, you will always find what you are looking for.

"Find something you love to do, your sweet spot. Don't settle. Keep searching. Believe and you will eventually find it."

11

Make Friends with Failure

Truly embracing this life lesson will change everything for you. It will transform the way you show up in the world each day. You will learn that no matter how badly you mess up, you cannot fail.

For a big chunk of my life, I viewed failure as a bad thing. I avoided it at all cost, always playing it safe. The last thing I wanted to be was a "failure", so I never pushed myself into situations where I wasn't sure if I would succeed or not. For a while operating like this was great. I always knew I would do well, whether at school or on the sports field, but deep down I knew I wasn't challenging myself. I was in my safe zone. The potential inside me was aching to get out (even though I didn't know what potential was at the time). I knew I wanted more for my life than to just get by.

Through studying successful people, reading biographies and getting good friends around me, I eventually started to push myself. At first it was intimidating as I was often the weakest in the class or on the team, but quickly I begin to learn from the new people around me. I raised my expectation levels, I worked smarter and most importantly I embraced failure. I learned it was just part of the process.

 This is the case for many people, until they realize that messing up and making mistakes is ok. Until people begin to understand that failure isn't a bad thing, they will always position themselves in situations where they are more likely to succeed than fail. We call this "staying in your comfort zone." It is nice and safe in your comfort zone. If you want a mediocre life, then existing in your comfort zone is fine, there is no shame in it; however, the fact you are reading this book about maximizing your potential make me assume you're not too interested in mediocrity.

Staying within your comfort zone is fine, but don't expect to improve that area of your life if that's where you choose to stay. You won't be stretched, nor will you experience any discomfort, or come face to face with failure – things needed to help you grow your potential.

"Value your relationship with failure because one day it will introduce you to success."

We all have a comfort zone in every area of our life, regardless of our level of talent. This is the sweet spot where you feel comfortable, where you feel safe and there is no risk of making a mistake or messing up. Whether we are talking about academics, music, sports, learning a new language, cooking, it doesn't matter. If you're going to maximize your potential, you're going to have to get comfortable with making mistakes and sometimes wiping out. Now, I'm not talking about mistakes that occur just because you're being sloppy or lazy. I'm referring to mistakes that come from you being stretched, from you having to dig deep and develop new skills and thought patterns. An example might be when you are learning a new language – at the beginning you are going to make lots of mistakes, however as you improve and master the language you'll make less errors.

Realizing that there is no such thing as failure in life is one of the most important things you can learn. One of the keys to success is knowing that everything that happens to you is just feedback from which you can learn and get better.

Once you begin to understand that failure doesn't really exist, the faster you can get out there and try new things without any fear.

Mistakes are like footprints leading you to success. They are full of valuable information that, if analyzed properly, can help us to quickly learn, get better, and move forward. Rather than seeing mistakes as a negative source of embarrassment, successful people use them as stepping stones to keep making progress.

Failure doesn't last forever. Of course it doesn't feel good at the time. It never does. But the people who can dust themselves off, learn, and get back on their feet, are the ones who are going to be successful.

Business start-ups, especially technology ones, pride themselves on "failing fast" — that is making as many mistakes as they can in the quickest time possible. They know that in their failings they find the vital knowledge that will project them towards success. Note: these are intelligent fails and risks, not just blind choices made without thinking.

These start-ups have a particular mindset in common. It's a mindset that says there is no failure, only feedback. It's knowing that no matter the result, you can find the positive in it and use the experience to catapult yourself even further forward.

"There is no failure only feedback."

Regardless of what you want to do in life, perseverance is key. There are going to be times when you want to give up and you feel like you cannot go on. People will tell you that you should quit, that it can't be done; but if you really want to do something, you're going to have to dig deep. You will need to be courageous and brave. The one thing you cannot do is quit.

Without wanting to confuse you or contradict myself, there are times in life when it is ok to quit or stop. This is discussed in a later chapter "Have the Courage to Make a Change."

12

The Future You

If you are committed to maximizing your potential and realizing your hopes and dreams, then you will need to keep growing as a person. Whatever you want to become in the future will require you to gain new skills, do things you've never done, meet people you've never met and step outside your comfort zone. Growing simply means you're getting better.

Our comfort zone is the place where we feel safe and comfortable. It is somewhere familiar to us all. You feel at ease and enjoy spending time hanging out here. Don't get me wrong, there is nothing wrong with having a comfort zone – in fact everyone should have a place where they can go and relax while recharging their batteries. But, if you are serious about becoming all you can be, you need to explore life outside this familiar place.

"The only way to grow and get better is to keep stepping outside of your comfort zone"

Just like when you arrive at a party and you don't know anyone's name, when you first leave your comfort zone it's going to be unfamiliar for you. It can be daunting and scary. Your natural tendency will be to retreat back to where you came from.

Maybe you can join a new lunchtime or after-school club. Is there an on-line course you take? (You'll find lots of free courses all over the internet, and YouTube is full of tutorials for literally anything). How about checking out your local library for a new book?

Stepping out of your comfort zone will look different for everyone. Do you have a passion for music? Perhaps you really love acting and performing? Are you a science lover? Whatever it is that gets you excited and in which-ever area of your life you want to grow, setting up camp in a new unchart-ed territory is something you're going to need to do.

Sure, people in your new zone might have more experience and be more advanced than you, however as you begin to get acquainted with you new surroundings and meet other like-minded people, you quickly begin to feel at ease in your new habitat. You'll learn from people's experience and from your mistakes; you will learn from other people and share their knowledge. If you want to grow, you've got to get out your comfort zone. **You can repeat or you can evolve.**

People who truly maximize their potential know that what was uncharted territory quickly becomes their new comfort zone. Once you are com-fortable, go and search out your next uncomfortable zone. Your potential to always improve never ends.

"Become the person you want to be."

13

Be the Most Positive Person You Know

Life is full of twists and turns. There will be good times, bad times, and challenging times. There will be moments when you feel unstoppable. Other times you'll want to curl up in bed and hide from the world. This is what we call the exciting rollercoaster of life!

The key to surviving these moments is in how you respond to life's challenges. Nobody is promised an easy life. Sure, some people are born with more advantages than others, but we all face challenges at some point in our life. I encourage you to stay positive and upbeat, knowing that the storms will always pass. Just hang on in there and don't give up. Focus on the positive things in your life and realize that all the other stuff is part of the learning curve. It's easy to become negative, very easy.

You choose how to view your current situation or circumstances. You can feel sorry for yourself, complain that life is unfair; or you can see all the good things in your life and the exciting potential that surrounds you.

You have the opportunity to be the most positive person you know. Nobody should be more positive than you. Your attitude and effort are the two things you can control in this big world of uncontrollables (we will discuss effort in a later chapter). Teach yourself that whatever happens to you is just part of the growth process. Responding to situations and learning from them, regardless of what actually happens to you, is what will define your future.

"Always believe something wonderful is about to happen."

Look for the gold in all situations. You've probably heard the saying that if someone gives you lemons, make lemonade, or if you find yourself in a puddle it is better to dance in it. I'm not talking about being someone who is annoyingly happy all the time, regardless of their current situation. Of course not. There are going to be times in your life when things don't turn out the way you wanted or expected. When this happens, it's ok to be upset, frustrated, sad. Do not, however, dwell in your disappointment and allow it to turn into negativity; you risk viewing everything through a pessimistic lens if you do so.

When people think of you, do they see you as a positive person that they want to be around? When your name flashes up on their phone, do they want to speak with you? Or do they want to run a mile away from your negative, pessimistic attitude?

It is easy to be negative. It hardly takes any effort. You can become a professional at it in no time. On the other hand, being positive is an intentional choice we make; it doesn't come without hard work. It takes practice. As humans, positivity isn't our default setting; yet you have the capability within you to change this.

Being positive will change the way you see the world. It allows you to see life in a completely different way. We can't control what happens in our lives, but we can control our attitude. **Be the most positive person you know.**

If you are a negative person, the exciting news is that you can change that. Since being negative is a habit, it will not be easy to change — but with focus and determination it is possible.

"Surround yourself with positive people and you'll quickly become a positive person."

You're going to need to limit your time around negative people. For some of you, these might be close friends or family members, maybe even your parents. I'm not saying cut them out of your life and never speak to them again. Rather, limit how much attention you pay to the negative things they say. Don't let negative people mar your life and dreams. Surround yourself with people who breathe life into you, who are optimistic, who believe in you.

1. Would you say that you are a positive person? Why?

2. How would your friends describe you?

3. Are you the type of friend you would want to call in a crisis?

4. Give an example of a setback you have experienced in life and how you responded to it.

5. How can you be more positive?

6. Do you have any friends or family members who are negative?

7. What can you do to limit the amount their negativity influences your life?

You Are an Original Masterpiece

The truth is that there is nobody like you. You are unique. You are an original masterpiece — a work of art. You have the opportunity to make your mark on the world through your gifts, talents and dreams.

Too many people buy into the lie that they do not have anything to give to society, or what they do have isn't worth sharing with the world. Instead, they choose to stay on the sidelines, to play it safe and keep all their gifts and uniqueness to themselves. They don't believe that they have anything to contribute.

Well I'm here to tell you that you are amazing. You are a limited edition. The world is waiting for you to step up and shine. Whether you have a passion to impact the world through great charity works, by your artistic flair, business, media, teaching, public servanthood, or by simply being an honest, loving, and ethical member of society, you can make a difference.

Pursue your passions and express yourself. Perhaps for you this is fighting against social injustices that break your heart. Or maybe it is creating opportunities for people who are in need. You may have an amazing business idea that is going to solve a huge problem. Whatever it is for you, be courageous. Be brave. Celebrate your originality. Shine bright and share your light with everyone around you. Don't water yourself down to fit into a neat little stereotype. Be you! Because you are amazing.

When you get to the end of your life, I hope you have poured it all out. I hope you have given it everything and left nothing on the shelf, giving the world the best of everything you have. If you've done this, regardless of anything else, you are a success.

"You are a **magnificent** work of art. You are far from **ordinary** or **average**."

15

What If?

You can either walk through life with very low expectations, worrying about all the things that might not go your way, being more concerned about what other people might think of you or you can have the mind-set of "what if....?" What if you really got serious about maximizing your potential? What if you committed yourself to improving a little bit each day? How far could you progress in a month? A year? 5 years? What if you chased your dreams, putting your fears aside, learning from your mistakes and being the very best you possible?

It is easier and more comfortable to take a route in life where you don't expect much. You can get away with being mediocre and settling for second best. If that's what you want for your life then that's absolutely fine — this is a judgement free zone.

The road of "What if?" is less traveled. It can often be lonely, frustrating, challenging, and messy. There will be times when you will want to turn back to an easier route. Yet the rewards of sticking it out and striving to fulfill your unique potential is more than worth it. Every dream starts with a "what if....?"

"What if you couldn't **fail**? What would **your** life look like?"

1. What would you do if you couldn't fail?

2. What would your dream life look like? Be as specific and detailed as possible. Try to visualize yourself living that life.

3. List any limiting beliefs that you have accepted into your life that have told you that something is impossible or too hard. (eg. I'm just not good enough, nobody in my family has done this, I don't have the finances...)

4. Once you have a list you can start the process of telling yourself that you are good enough and that things aren't impossible. Note: this takes time so I encourage you to review the list as often as you can to reprogram your limiting beliefs.

"Dare to dream."

16

Hard Work is Your Best Friend

No matter how hard we try, we can't control what happens to us. One thing we can control is our effort level. Other people might have more natural talent than you; however, there is no reason why they should be working harder than you.

Too many people rely on their talent alone, and never develop the skill of working hard. Eventually, people who rely solely on their talent stop growing and improving. They plateau because they have not developed their work ethic. Don't let this be you. Develop the habit of always giving 100% effort, no matter how difficult things get. I guarantee you will quickly see huge progress.

"You cannot control many things in life; but you have 100% control of your effort and attitude."

Build a reputation for being someone who gives 100% effort all the time. Be persistent. Day in and day out, not just when you feel like it. Nobody can take away your work ethic.

In a world where most people think success comes easily, and any sign of a challenge means they simply give up, consistent effort is the thing that is going to set people apart. If you work hard you will always give yourself a chance.

"With effort, anything is possible."

17

You Do You

You are unique. More unique than you'll ever know. You have your own DNA. You have your own fingerprints. You speak in a different way than anyone else. You smile like nobody else. More importantly, you have your own way of interpreting the world and the life around you. Nobody does you like you!

So why do so many people try to be like someone else? Why are there so many people that feel the need to copy other people's opinions, tastes in music, fashion, sense of humor, or political viewpoints? The answer is this: it takes courage to be yourself. It is much easier, safer, and more comfortable to follow the crowd — there's no risk of anyone questioning you.

Don't get me wrong, safety can be a good thing. When crossing the street or playing with matches, safety should be your number one concern; but when we are talking about maximizing your potential, safety is certainly not your friend.

"Have confidence and be courageous."

Your life journey has made you into the person you are today. Your upbringing, your childhood, where you live, your parents, your friends, the books you read — whether your experience was positive or negative — they all have an effect on who you are and how you show up in the world. There will never be another YOU! God broke the mold when He made you. This is something to be celebrated not hidden.

I want to encourage you to enjoy being you! You owe it to yourself. The world is waiting for you to show up. Share your passions, thoughts, opinions, and sense of humor with everyone — pour it out! We want to know you! Please don't buy into the lie that you need to be just like everyone else. Be confident in being you. There is only one!

As you experience more of this life, and you meet new people along the way, your opinions, tastes and perspectives will change. You'll see the world through new, different lenses. This is perfectly normal and part of the growing process.

Be yourself and share all that you are becoming! You were born to shine brightly. What are you waiting for?

"Don't **follow** the crowd. You do you like no one else. Share your **passions, talents** and **gifts**. The world is waiting for you."

18

Patience

Spend some time flicking through a magazine or surfing social media and you will be sure to stumble over the promise of tips on how to achieve something fast: Olympic level fitness in 7 days, learn native level Mandarin in 3 weeks, get rich quick etc. These types of promises catch our attention because we'd all like to get maximum results from the least effort possible. Who wouldn't?

The truth is that life doesn't work like that. Everything takes time. And there is beauty in that. It is all about the journey. It is a roller coaster of ups and downs, twists and turns, discoveries and setbacks. There are no get rich quick schemes that work, and there are no shortcuts to being successful. The secret is patience, and lots of it.

"Hard work and patience: the two most vital ingredients to success."

Patience is a dying art. It is slow but it is most certainly a 'doing' word. Just like an athlete works on their speed, you need to work on your patience. People don't like to wait. They are impatient. They want their food, coffee, internet and everything else NOW! Confession time: I hate to wait. So, in a world that seems to be getting faster and faster, I want to encourage you to be patient.

Patience's best friend is persistence. Be persistent. The two go hand in hand. Don't give up because you are not immediately achieving what you want. Giving up is easy. The high and lows, the frustrations, the dashed hopes, they are all part of the process. This is life's way of teaching you. Embrace the waiting. Dig in when you feel like giving up. Most people quite — but not you.

Don't try to run before you can walk. Babies learn what they need to from crawling so when they do attempt a full-on toddler walk they have a greater chance of staying on their feet. The life-skills you are learning along your personal journey will help you as you move closer to your goals and dreams. Cutting corners isn't an option. Be patient.

"A life well lived is a mixture of mistakes, learning, reflection, waiting, growing, patience, and hard work."

19

Learn to Listen

Human beings are designed to connect with each other. Speaking with other humans is how we do this. It is known as having a conversation, in person, face to face. Yes, conversation, NOT texts, posts, likes, comments or tweets. Shock horror!

A conversation is a two-way process. You speak and you listen. It is not just about you voicing your opinion or unloading everything within you. Being able to converse is a skilled endeavor, yet it is an art form that everybody can learn.

Focus on the listening part of conversations. Talking is easy. Learn to listen. This is a life skill that will propel you towards fulfilling your potential. An astute listener focuses solely on what the person is saying and the way they are saying it. They listen to the inflection in the speaker's voice and tune into the speaker's emotions. Listeners aren't distracted by their phones, texting, playing games, or stray pigeons. They aren't preparing and thinking about their response while the other person is speaking. No — they are LISTENING and keeping up with the conversation. Once the person has finished speaking, then you can speak. You'll now have all the facts and be in a much better position to reply. The other person will feel heard and understood. Your friends will appreciate that you took the time to truly listen. You will learn so much more, too. Two ears, one mouth: use them proportionally and watch your relationships soar.

"You learn from listening, not talking."

1. Why is listening to others so important?

2. How do you feel when you know somebody is listening closely when you are speaking?

3. Why is listening to others difficult sometimes?

4. What are some things we can do to make others feel like we're really listening to them? Practice with a friend.

20

Fit for Purpose

If the idea of gym class at school gives you the shivers and the mention of any type of running makes you immediately feel sick, then getting fit probably isn't something that you can get excited about. On the whole, being forced to do sport or physical activity at school — unless you're in the superhuman elite club who is good at every type of sport — will most probably make you want to avoid physical activity at all costs.

Exercise actually makes you feel more energized. If you want to achieve a lot with your life, you're going to need have the energy to keep you going. Getting in shape and keeping fit can be fun (it really can!) There are activities for everyone that can help you get fit and that you will enjoy. If you are committed to getting in shape, it is up to you to find an activity that you enjoy, and that most importantly gets you up and moving.

Science shows that exercise releases 'feel good endorphins' into our bloodstream that can instantly change the mood you are in. Just going for a walk and getting blood flowing through your body can make you feel totally different, especially if you are feeling 'stuck' or 'frustrated'.

"Maximizing your potential is never easy. If you don't have the energy you need you will struggle to make real progress."

If you cannot stand running, don't run. If you don't like the smell of chlorine and the thought of wearing bathing suits freaks you out, don't go swimming. Do something you enjoy that is going to get your heart rate up. It might be lifting weights, dancing, cycling, walking, rollerblading, rock climbing, rowing — whatever you are going to have fun doing and won't dread. Mix things up, too, so your workouts are something you look forward to. Do something new, listen to music or a podcast, invite friends, have some fun!

Believe it or not, you'll have more energy once you make regular exercise part of your life. If you are serious about making progress on your goals and realizing your dreams, it's going to be much tougher if your energy levels are so low that you struggle to get out of bed. As you exercise more and you start to feel all the benefits that working out gives you, you'll find it hard to live without it. You'll sleep like a newborn baby and enjoy being in much better moods. Chances are you'll live longer too.

Getting fit can be whatever you want it to be. You don't have to sign up for a marathon or transatlantic swim. Explore new things, find out what works for you. Just start, no matter your current physical shape or level of fitness. Once you get into a routine, you'll make it a part of who YOU are and what you do.

ACTIONABLE TIPS FOR GETTING FIT:

1. Just start. First step is to get your body moving and your heart pumping. Simply get yourself moving, even if just to start with it is going walking around the block.

2. Look for clubs or groups you can join. You'll meet new people too.

3. Get a friend to workout with. You will motivate each other to stick at it.

4. Try something new. Look online for new activities.

5. If you don't enjoy the activity, quit and keep searching until you find something you enjoy.

6. It is easier to stay in shape than to try to get back in shape. Try to exercise for 45 minutes, 3 times per week. It is important to raise your heart rate as you exercise. You be able to breathe normally, but should not be able to hold a full on conversation. If you can you probably aren't working your heart enough (check with a medical or fitness professional for more information here).

7. Don't be too hard on yourself. Developing new habits can be tough. It'll be worth it in the end.

8. The internet is your friend here: look for different activities and work-out plans that interest you.

21

Organize Your Potential

One of the biggest pieces of advice I can give to you is get organized. Life is challenging enough as it is without us making it even harder for ourselves by being disorganized. Living in a state of constant chaos is stressful. Once you're organized, you won't need to be worrying all the time about where things are, where you need to be, or other important things. Your mind can switch off and relax. By being organized you'll feel much more in control. You will have more time to focus on the important things that will allow you to keep pushing ahead.

So, what does being organized look like? Well, this is different for us all. For starters, I would say that having your school work schedules and files in order is most important. Make sure you know the time of your classes, the location, homework and project deadlines. Often you can get a list of projects and coursework for the semester, or even the entire year from your teachers — this allows you to plan ahead and allocate time to study and complete the required work on time.

Aim to have your workbooks, notes and files in order. Use file dividers and page markers to help you. You'll find it much easier to revise and study for tests. If you use a computer, digitally set your files up in an orderly manner so you can quickly find notes.

Once you've got your school work in order you can start to focus on other areas of your life — clothes, bedroom etc. **Getting organized isn't glamorous. It sounds boring and dull. To some extent it is; but if you're serious about being successful and maximizing your potential then**

this is non-negotiable. As you get older, as you have may already started to notice, life puts more demands on your time. Not only will you have more school work to do, but you'll also have other grown-up responsibilities that you need to stay on top of, like bank statements, jobs, chores, or family.

Getting organized can seem extremely daunting, especially if your current life is the exact opposite of order. Start small and focus on one area of your life (I recommend your academics). Once you prove to yourself that you can keep this area organized, move onto another area. Soon, being organized will be a way of life — a core habit of yours . You will feel empowered and be ready for any challenge life can throw at you.

"If you **fail** to plan, you are **planning** to fail."

Nowadays there are hundreds of apps and software programs available to help organize your life. Most email providers have online calendars you can use and sync up with your phone to begin managing your time. Also, Evernote (evernote.com) is a fantastic tool that allows you to file and store notes, documents, coursework, etc. and then easily search for it (there is a free and premium option).

So be organized. Your 'future you' will thank you for it.

List one area of your life where you can become more organized:

What is a next step you can take to start getting your life in order?

22

Put Your Phone Down

Cell Phones are an integral part of our lives these days. It's hard to imagine life without them. Nearly everything we do these days is on a mobile phone — texting, emailing, posting, playing, scrolling, liking, ordering, posing for selfies. If you've ever lost your phone you know the feeling of thinking your world is about to collapse around you. I want to encourage you to not get so consumed by your phone that you'll miss life going on around you.

There is nothing worse than meeting up with a friend and all they do is keep checking their phone. If you're going to agree to spend time with someone, surely you can put your phone down? You're not going to miss anything for 30 minutes. Put your phone away. Put it in your pocket or in your bag. Don't leave it on the table — unless you are waiting for an EXTREMELY important life-or-death call regarding your sick hamster. Take a break from social media or whatever the latest craze is when you are reading this. Instead, really focus on who you are talking to. You'll be amazed at how much better the conversation will be and how much more fun you'll have if you are fully engaged. Plus, it's just bad manners to be on your phone. Developing the skills to become a great listener will transform your world.

As humans, we are designed to communicate with each other. Don't get me wrong, a world with cell phones is way better than a medieval world that communicates via messengers or carrier pigeon; but try to limit the amount of time your face is stuck staring at your phone. You'll begin to be so much more aware of what is going on around you.

"Life is what happens when your cellphone is charging."

You can download apps that monitor and report how long you spend using your phone each day. I challenge you to measure this for a week — the following week dedicate the exact same amount of time to something that is going to help you maximize your potential.

23

Speak to New People

Having a close circle of friends is great, especially when you all have common, shared interests. Yet, if you only ever talk and spend time with certain friends, you are only ever going to hear certain opinions or learn about certain things. There is nothing wrong with maintaining a tight friend network, but always look to speak with new people. Take time and be intentional about conversing with people you've never connected with before. You'll learn so much more, and your perspective will be greatly enhanced.

Next time you get the opportunity to speak to an older person you should definitely take advantage. Many young people think that they have nothing to learn from old people; however, if you stop and listen, you'll realize that you can gain lots of wisdom from them. They've lived and experienced life, picking up wisdom and understanding along the way. **Find out what they've learned about life and what advice they would give their younger self. Borrow their wisdom, broaden your thinking and get ahead of everybody else.**

"Keep **searching** for new people to speak to. One conversation can change **everything** — the way you **think**, the way you **view** the world, the way you view **yourself**."

24

Choose Your Friends Wisely

Having friends can be one of the best experiences in life. Friends are like family, only you get to choose them. As you grow and gain a better understanding of yourself and the direction you want to go in life, the friends around you will become even more important.

We all want friends who are there to celebrate the good times, to encourage us and to cheer us up when we are down. These are the type of friends we need and should desire. But sometimes our friends can be exactly the opposite of what we need. When this happens, it can be hard.

Our natural instinct tells us that having people in our life who we like, trust and have spent a good portion of our life with should be a good thing — yet this is not always the case. It may be that certain friends have different plans for their lives, or worse, no plan at all. They can start to be a bad influence on you, directly and indirectly.

"Introduce me to your friends and I'll introduce you to your future."

Some friends will start to see you getting focused on maximizing your potential and they won't like it. It might make them feel inferior or uncomfortable. They can quickly become jealous and start to tell you that realizing your dreams is only for the movies, that you're kidding yourself if you think you'll ever amount to something. What they don't understand is that anybody can maximize their potential if they focus and work hard. You need to prepare yourself for their jealousy and other bad influences.

At first you might not notice it, but over time they can get you off track and distract you. This isn't necessarily a bad thing if you don't plan much for your life, but if you do want to make the most of it, then this is something you will need to address.

Every situation is different, however, if you find yourself hanging out with people who are taking you down paths that you know you shouldn't be going, then it's time for a "friend review". This doesn't mean you just instantly stop seeing your friends overnight; instead, start to reduce the amount of time you spend with them gradually. This way you can still be friends with them, but they won't have such an impactful influence in your life.

And for those of you who may be thinking that this is a little intense, you're right, it is. If you're serious about being successful, you simply can't afford to risk being taken off course.

"You can't **soar** like an **eagle** if you surround yourself with **turkeys**"

Friends should encourage you to maximize your potential and to make the most out of your gifts. Ask yourself the following questions:

- Do my friends build me up?

- Do they encourage me?

- Are they honest with me?

- Do they challenge me to be the best I can possibly be? Or are they negative and pessimistic?

- Are they taking me in the direction I want to go?

- How do they affect my thinking?

25

University of Life

People I've met who strive to maximize their potential are all learners. They don't just do the bare minimum that they need to pass a test or exam at school. They are curious, thirsty for knowledge. The things they learn are all different and don't always have any relation to what they are studying at school. They love to learn and discover new things across all areas of life.

I encourage you to do the same! Be a lifelong learner. Enroll yourself into the University of Life — tuition is free. If you like reading, then head to your local library and pick up a book on a topic you want to know more about. You'll be surprised how quickly you'll learn, and then you have all this new information that will give you a whole new perspective on the world. Read biographies of people you think were successful. Learn how they approached life and applied themselves to achieving their own goals and dreams.

Don't like reading? No problem. You can borrow audiobooks from most libraries to listen on your phone or computer. Download podcasts. Or you can watch TED (www.ted.com) or Google talks (talksat.withgoogle.com) online — here you'll find thousands of interesting topics. You have so much information from people who have gone before you and who are willing to share all their wisdom available at your fingertips, it is mind-blowing.

"Success is no accident. It is where hard work, perseverance, learning, studying, and sacrifice all come together."

Once you get a taste for learning, everything changes. You'll want to know more and discover everything. Trust me, everyone will want you on their quiz team!

Let me put it this way: it's fine if you're just going to do the bare minimum reading from school, or you're only interested in celebrity gossip, sports results, or social media, but don't expect to maximize your potential.

More importantly, know that one idea or inspiring story that you read or listen to can change your life in an instant. You might read something that completely changes your perspective or motivates you to do something you never thought possible. You never know when you're going to come across that one idea or thought. Playing video games or catching up on the latest celebratory wedding isn't going to give you that life changing insight. Do yourself a favor. Be a lifelong learner.

Plus, learning new things makes you interesting. You'll have fresh things to talk about and share with your friends. No one wants to hang around someone who is boring!

"Invest in yourself. Become a lifelong learner. You can always improve and get better."

26

No Regrets

When you are younger and starting out in life, the statement "no regrets" is a little less relevant. Yet as people get older and the years begin to pass more and more quickly, you will start to look back and reflect over your life. Hopefully you will not have regrets, or dwell on the things you never did, the risks you never took, the dreams you never chased, all the unfulfilled potential still inside you. Regrets hurt. Unfulfilled potential is a heavy burden to carry around.

Don't put yourself through the misery of living with unfulfilled potential. Instead set out, from today, to give life everything you've got. As my dad used to tell me, "Son, it's not a dress rehearsal." Work hard, dream big and don't give up. Ignore those who tell you to settle.

Please do not put yourself in the position where you wished you'd made more of your life or the opportunities you were given. The only way to avoid having any regrets is to take action, today.

"Give life your best shot. Ignore those that tell you to settle for average. That's not the life for you."

Looking back over your life in 10, 20, 30, or even 60 years and wishing you had tried harder, spent less time in your comfort zone, been braver or gone after your dreams, that will not be fun. Thinking what could have been will only fill you with disappointment and pain.

Even if life doesn't work out the way you might have wanted it, at least you'll have the satisfaction of knowing that you gave it your all. You used up everything you had. Promise yourself that you won't look back over your life and regret not trying to become the best you could possibly be.

How would you feel if you got to the end of your life and you hadn't pursued your dreams or worse, even made an attempt to go after them?

What can you do to make sure you do to fulfill your potential?

"Looking back over your life in twenty years, you will be more disappointed by the things that you didn't do than by the ones you did. Just go for it!"

27

Help Please!

One of the biggest misunderstandings is the idea of a "self-made man or woman". The media tells us all the time about people who have overcome adversity, challenges and a humble background to be successful. These people are celebrated for achieving amazing things. We are led to believe that they did it all on their own, standing up against all the odds and coming out victorious on the other side. Yet, if you take the time to study successful people, you will realize that nobody is self-made. Yes, they might have worked extremely hard and handled some exceptionally tough circumstances, but they didn't achieve everything on their own.

Behind every successful person you'll find someone who has helped them along the way. Successful people are too smart to try and achieve everything on their own. Why waste time and effort trying and struggling to work something out on your own when you can ask the help of someone else?

If you haven't worked this out yet, you soon will: human beings are extremely proud. We don't like to ask for help. Rather, we like to struggle along in the false hope that we'll eventually work it out.

"Don't be too **proud** to ask for help. That's not bravery; it is **foolishness**."

As humans we like to give everybody the impression that we've got it all worked out, we know exactly what we are doing, and we know where we are going. It's a trait that we learn quickly pretty much after birth. Babies like to show they can do things on their own and can become stubborn very quickly! This stubbornness is also referred to as our ego. Naturally we don't like to show our weaknesses because we think people may think less of us or laugh at us.

Successful people are never too proud to ask for help. They realize that they simply cannot know everything. They understand that everybody was a beginner once. They are prepared to admit when they are unsure of what to do. Rather than wasting time making silly mistakes, they lean on the wisdom of other people who have gone down the path before them. Moving their pride and ego aside, they search out others who can help them or who can offer wise counsel. Once you get over the fear that someone may realize you don't know what you're doing, or that you are a beginner (shock horror!) you will start to make much faster progress. You can avoid the mistakes and pitfalls that inevitably lie ahead by utilizing the experiences of others.

As you start to seek out people who may be able to help you navigate the paths of life, you will be amazed at how many want to help you. Look to build a team of people around you that you can trust and to whom you can go for advice. This may include family members, but could really involve anybody. All of a sudden, everything will not seem as daunting. You'll be able to stand on the shoulders of giants and see way down the road ahead of you. You'll be rocketing towards your dreams and goals.

"Help comes to those who have the courage and wisdom to ask for it."

28

Look the Part

Looking the part is all about making an effort and preparing yourself. I believe that we should all do what we can to make ourselves as presentable as possible. Take a shower, bathe or wash. Every day. Comb your hair. Brush your teeth. If you struggle with bad breath invest in some mouthwash and carry mints with you. Wear antiperspirant (everyone will thank you). Ensure your clothes are clean and neat. Dress appropriately for the occasion. Polish your shoes. Remember to smile.

Doing this you will make you more confident. Prepare yourself to be successful. You don't necessarily need to stand out from the crowd by being over-groomed or overdressed, but you certainly don't want to stand out for your poor hygiene or looking too scruffy.

Please don't confuse this with vanity. You don't need to look like you've just stepped off the nearest catwalk or walked straight out of a hair salon. Neither do you need to spend money on designer clothes or the latest fashions. All you really need to do is make an effort and take some pride in your appearance. People will notice and will realize that you are committed to being successful. Make sure people remember you for what you say, not for your eye-watering bad breath.

If you act successful in all areas of your life, sooner or later it will become your normal behavior. Have high standards of excellence across all areas of your life. Look the part.

"If you take care of the **small** things the **big** things will take care of themselves."

29

Be On Time

I learned timekeeping from my dad. He was a fireman and always used to remind us that if he was late to a fire people would die. Yeah, quite a tough life lesson to learn aged 7 – but it worked. I was never late for school. Since then I've strived to always be on time for everything. You should too.

You see, getting somewhere on time says so many things. Firstly, it says that you respect the person you are meeting or the place you are going. Even if you are meeting a friend you've known for years, it says that you are committed and that you care.

Secondly, it massively reduces stress. Being late for something means you are rushing. You are constantly checking your watch and causing yourself undue pressure. You can't enjoy the journey. Not being on time means you are chasing time instead of being in control of your agenda.

I used to work in the recruitment industry helping recent college graduates get jobs with companies. If someone was late to our first meeting and they did not call ahead to say they would not be on time, then, regardless of how good, clever, or smart they were, we knew we couldn't risk recommending them to our clients. Simply put: we couldn't trust them. Build a reputation for being on time.

"Being **punctual** says everything about you. Set yourself up for **success** — be on time"

Tips for being on time:

1. Plan in advance. Get everything you need ready before-hand — especially if you are meeting someone first thing in the morning.

2. Always allow additional time (especially if you are using public transport or there is bad weather)

3. If you need to be somewhere in the morning make sure you go to bed early the night before.

4. Repeat. If you need to be somewhere in the afternoon, make sure you go to bed early the night before. We all need more sleep

5. Place your alarm clock on the other side of your room. Pressing snooze is too easy.

6. If you are going to be late, let whoever you are meeting know at least 15 minutes in advance.

7. Apologize if you're late. It shows you respect that person's time.

30

Acknowledge People

When I was 13, I went on an adventure holiday trip to the South of France with my school. We went canoeing, windsurfing and sailing in the Mediterranean Sea. It was amazing, except a few days in I got really sick and had to go to the doctor's office with heat stroke. That wasn't much fun. In fact, it was pretty terrible.

The thing I remember best from visiting the doctor is that it was really busy in the small waiting room with about 12 chairs facing each other. Each person who entered went around the room and said "bonjour" (good day) to every single person. Despite feeling horrendous and on the verge of throwing up, I was still mesmerized by it. It's something that I will never forget. At first, I thought they were joking! I loved the fact that people acknowledged other human beings with a simple but powerful "good morning". It was humanity at its best.

These days, with technology playing such a huge role in our lives, it is easy to miss the other humans around us. Today we are so connected that we can feel disconnected. We communicate so much by texting and emails that people can just pass us by. We get used to not acknowledging other humans. It seems we are always in a rush to get somewhere that we forget that we share the planet with others.

"People remember how you treat them. As humans we all need to be respected."

As fast, powerful and efficient as technology can be, nothing can compare to the uniqueness of a fellow human. Don't miss that or lose sight of it. Always take the time to acknowledge people when you enter a room. It doesn't need to be a big fanfare; a simple hello, good morning (or similar) will do. Maybe a handshake or a hug if you know them well. Even if you're shy, tired, or simply don't feel like it.

This little act of acknowledgement is huge. As you start to do it, you'll start to realize the amazing array of other human beings that you share planet earth with. You'll begin to notice the unique qualities and gifts within other people, which in turn will remind you of your own unique potential. Always acknowledge people.

"Treat people the way you would like to be treated."

31

Be Intentional

Have you gotten to the end of a day and you thought, "Wow, what did I do today? Where did the time go?" Usually, this means you were not intentional with your time.

In order to maximize your potential, you're going to need to be intentional with both your time, and your actions. Everything you do should have a purpose. If not, you start to drift in directions that are often not where you want to go.

Time – be intentional with your time. We all have 24 hours each day available to us. Use it wisely and productively. Life has many distractions that can make you think you're moving forwards just because you're busy, but don't mistake busyness for productivity. Be intentional about your schedule each day. For example, set aside time to study — don't use it to check social media. Allocate time to watch tv, schedule time to see friends, etc. This might sound too regimented for some people and if so, that's absolutely fine, you don't have to do it. However, if you are serious about maximizing the gifts and talents you've been blessed with, then I seriously encourage you to invest in this. If you don't, your time will run away from you. Your days will run away from you. Eventually your life will start to run away from you. You'll only operate at average capacity and end up living an average life.

Decisions – be intentional with your decision making. When making a big decision that will have a long-term impact on your future (not decisions like what color socks to wear today) you should be asking yourself if the choice will take you closer or further away from where you want to get to. If you're not careful, you can find yourselves making long term decisions with a short-term mindset— this almost always takes you away from where you really want to be.

Being intentional isn't about being serious all the time and extracting the fun out of everything. It's about being aware that the choices and decisions we make each and every day have consequences. In fact, through being intentional about our life we can actually free ourselves up to have even more fun. Through being aware of the direction we are trying to go, we can relax and enjoy the ride a lot more without worrying all the time. We are able to stop fretting about getting knocked off track because we know what we are focusing on. If we aren't careful and mindful of where we want to be going, we can find ourselves a long way from the path we want our life to be on. Be intentional.

"Effort and courage are not enough if you don't have purpose and direction."

32

Manners Please!

If manners were animals, they would be on the endangered species list. No matter the status, the position, the wealth, the fame, or the possessions you acquire in life, without manners it all counts for nothing.

Human beings distinguish themselves from the animal kingdom by the respect, courtesy and politeness that we express to one another. Head down to your local zoo and you won't see the penguins apologizing for splashing their neighbors in the pool. Neither will you hear many "pleases" or "thank yous" among the lions at feeding time.

Manners demonstrate that we value and honor other people. They also show that we are grateful for what we have and the opportunities we are given. More importantly, they symbolize how you feel about yourself inside. They show that you respect yourself and others.

The other great thing about having manners is that you can easily set yourself apart from everyone else. Manners are so rare these days that by simply treating people with respect you will stand out from the crowd. Now, I am not saying be polite so you can get something in return. No, be polite because it is the right thing to do; the rest is a bonus.

Manners tell people that you respect them. Ensure you always say "please" and thank you". Show the person you appreciate them. Even though you cannot measure it, by you being polite you can encourage others to have manners too. Imagine how much more enjoyable life would be if everyone displayed manners and treated each other with respect!

"Good **manners** are just a way of showing other people that we **respect** them."

Different cultures do have different manners. But overall, I'd say the following provide a pretty good manners baseline for every human sharing planet earth:

1. Treat people the way you'd want to be treated.
2. Say "Please."
3. Say "Thank You."
4. Say "Sorry," or "Excuse me."
5. Say "Good Morning/ Afternoon/ Evening."
6. Let people know you appreciate them.
7. Look people in the eye when you're speaking with them.
8. Put your phone away.
9. Stop looking at your phone.
10. Upon meeting someone shake their hand.

"**Manners** don't cost you anything. They are your **free** ticket to the world."

33

How Would You Like to Be Remembered?

Life is not a competition to see who can achieve or acquire the most things or prizes. Too many people have already tried that and found it to be a lonely, miserable road. When you get to the end of your life, at your funeral, people won't be talking about how much money you had, the number of college degrees you received, the car your drove, or if you even fulfilled your potential. They will be talking about how you made them feel and what you did for others.

Hear me correctly on this: I'm not saying that these things are not important. I am not saying you should not go out and try to maximize your potential. No. I am saying that being a high achiever, maximizing your potential, and being successful will not mean anything if you have not positively impacted the people around you. Perhaps it is through your kindness, or through your compassion. Maybe it is through the passion you had for life, or your ability to always believe the best in people. There is no right answer here. You must work out the right answer for yourself. How will you be remembered?

If you are truly focused on maximizing your potential and becoming the best you can be, then you should also be inspiring others to do the same with their lives along the way. Become so excited and hopeful for life that people want to be around you. Help others on their journey. Share with them the wisdom you learn. Encourage, inspire, and motivate them.

"While you are busy maximizing your **potential**, don't forget about the world around you. Encourage, inspire and help others along the way."

34

Get Some Sleep

Sleep is underrated. Telling someone to go to bed earlier is never going to be popular. Staying up late is apparently what cool people do so that they won't miss out on any of life's action. The truth is, not getting enough sleep is what keeps you from maximizing your potential. Sleep is powerful and essential if you're serious about realizing all your potential. Here are the key benefits of sleep and why you should be getting at least 7-8 hours per night taken from the journal – 'Sleep' (published 2010):

i.   Improves your memory

ii.   Puts you in a better mood and enhances optimism

iii. Increases your creativity

iv.   Sharpens your attention span

v.   Gives your body time to replenish and grow

vi.   Helps maintain a healthy metabolism

vii. Reduces stress levels

viii. Increases energy

Getting enough sleep ensures you are prepared mentally and physically to press on. It is vital to be in the right mindset and have the energy to run at life with all you have. Without enough sleep, you will constantly fight an upward battle and not give yourself the best possible chance for success.

Going to bed at a time that allows you to fully rest and rejuvenate takes practice. You need to be dedicated and intentional, and there will always be distractions. Yet, if you can ignore these distractions and consistently get 8 hours of sleep or more per night, you will give yourself the best possible chance to succeed.

"Don't sleepwalk into an *average* life."

35

It's All About the Money

Wherever you go, no matter what you do, you cannot avoid money. It is part of life.

To be clear: money certainly doesn't make you happy. Just ask all the miserable rich folks out there. But not having money can also make you very unhappy — especially if it leads you to a life that is constrained by the shackles of debt.

Unfortunately, most schools do not teach the mechanics behind how money works. We are left to learn about money from parents, friends or pets; for most of us that means no financial education at all.

One of the biggest secrets about handling money and finances is that it is not as difficult as the world will have you believe. Anybody who has a desire to learn can do so. Wall Street will have you believe that you need to be a finance guru to understand the complexities of money; however, this is only so they can charge you crazy fees for their advice.

"Mastering money is more about habits than money itself."

Understanding how money works is something that we can all achieve. If you learn to understand and master money, you will be able to avoid a lot of pain and stress. It's a mindset that allows you to be in control of your money, instead of money controlling you. Being ignorant and believing it is only for rich kids isn't going to help you. I have no idea why financial literacy is not taught in every single school. The earlier you can learn the principles that surround money the better.

Don't try to avoid money, or think that only rich people or financial experts in suits know how it works. Burying your head in the sand isn't going to help you. It'll only numb the inevitable pain that will come your way if you don't get smart about money. If you come from a family who will help you to learn about money, or perhaps you receive financial education at school, utilize these opportunities as much as you can. However, if you're like me and you didn't receive any guidance, advice, or training on how to handle money, then you're going to need to teach yourself. Read some books, listen to some podcasts, watch some YouTube videos, ask people you respect for some advice (or someone they can recommend you talk to). I have also listed some resources for you at the end of this chapter. Check them out!

Most often, the number one cause of stress in people's' lives is money. People worry about not having enough money and people worry that when they have enough that it might run out. Too many people let money control their lives. It's like a rollercoaster.

Another key to being successful (and alleviating stress and worry) is to take control of your money. It will bring you peace to focus on the things you want to focus on without having to worry about your next paycheck or not being able to afford things you want.

Right now, you may or may not earn any money. Some of you might have part-time jobs or you might get paid from doing chores, walking dogs or babysitting. Whether you are earning now or not you soon will be. **You are never too young to educate yourself about money.**

When I say educate yourself about money, I'm not talking complex, PhD level principles — these are simple, straight forward ideas anyone can start to apply. By all means, if complex financial concepts interest you and get you excited, then go for it. You see, the things I've learned about money are:

1. You cannot spend more than you earn — use a budget to help you manage and track your spending. Know where your money is being spent. This is your first step to getting in control of your money.

2. Learn the difference between a need and a want. The less wants you have the more money you will have.

3. Avoid debt and carrying a credit card balance.

4. Build towards saving an emergency fund to cover 3 months of living expenses. This prevents you from needing to borrow money or use a credit card. It proves to yourself that you have the discipline to save, and it will give you peace of mind should you encounter an "emergency".

5. Having money saved up will mean you have options. You won't need to take the first job that you come across because you have to, it will give you freedom to choose what you want to do.

6. Take responsibility for saving. Don't rely on your parents or family to give you money. If they do, then great; focus instead on taking ownership of your own financial situation.

7. Save 15% (at least) of everything you earn and invest in the stock market (see list of book and resources below for advice on this). The more you can save the better.

8. Keep your living costs as low as possible. For most of you reading this book this will not be relevant right now, as you most probably live at home; however, as you get older try to keep your costs as low as possible. Avoid the need to impress others or gain approval from buying the latest gadgets, most expensive sneakers or shiniest phone. This will mean you have more money to save and invest.

9. Learn about and utilize compound interest. Learn why it should be your best friend. See how over time your money can start to earn money for you while you sleep (literally). This principle is core to building real wealth. The quicker you can familiarize yourself with compound interest the faster it can start working for you.

10. Don't bury your head in the sand hoping for the best — educate yourself.

11. Invest your money for the future.

Again, let's be very clear: money <u>will not</u> make you happy. Yet, if you can begin to save and invest at an early age, you are going to be in a much better position to make decisions that you want to make, rather than being forced into doing things or taking jobs that you might not want to. Having money (at least 1 year of living expenses) gives you freedom. It prevents you from ever being tied to a job or a paycheck.

Lastly: please understand that you do not need to be earning millions and millions of dollars each year to create a secure financial platform for yourself. There are too many bankrupt sport stars to prove this to be true. You only need to earn enough money where you can save a portion of your income (at least 15%, but ideally more), invest it in the stock market (I recommend low-cost index funds – you can read more from the resources listed below) and allow your money to start working for you.

Resources to kick start your financial education:

Books (most local libraries will have these):

Simple Path to Wealth – J.L. Collins

The Little Book of Common Sense Investing – John C. Bogle

Millionaire Next Door – Thomas J. Stanley & William D. Danko

Your Money or Your Life – Vicki Robin

Websites:

High School Financial Planning Program – www.hsfpp.org

ChooseFI – www.choosefi.com

Get Rich Slowly – www.getrichslowly.org

Next Gen Personal Finance – www.ngpf.org

"By educating yourself, you have the power to **choose** whether you allow **money** to control you, or you **control** your money."

36

Have the Courage to Make a Change

Ok, so you've defined your own version of success and you've started to plan your life with the end in mind, you're now moving forward. You've got some traction. Nevertheless, if you find that you aren't enjoying what you are pursuing, whether that's an academic course, a job, an apprentice-ship, whatever it may be, please have the courage to stop.

Listen very closely here: I am not saying give up and throw in the towel at your first taste of adversity or your first bump in the road. Certainly not. I am saying that if you have pursued something for a decent period of time and you can honestly say that this route is not for you, having given it your fullest effort, then have the courage to reassess and change.

> "Make sure your ladder is leaning against a tree you want to climb."

Changing direction isn't often straightforward. It's messy, it's time con-suming, emotionally draining, and most often will cost you money. Again, it is something that shouldn't be taken lightly. Please don't have the mind-set that you can just quit anything you do whenever you're having a bad day or week. Changing your direction should be something that is taken very seriously, and should certainly not be something that is done often. This is why determining what you want to pursue is so important.

But if you do make a decision that you later regret or feel doesn't suit you, and you can honestly say you've tried, then it's ok to change. Do not feel you have to stick to something that doesn't appeal to you just to please your parents or your family.

Equally, do not feel you need to grin and bear something just to prove to people that you are not a quitter. There is no shame in holding your hand up and saying that whatever it is you started isn't for you. Be true to yourself even if your family tries to talk you out of it. Learn from the experience and utilize it to help you refine what it is that you would rather be doing. Life is too short to do something you're not enjoying or that you can't see a future in.

Believe me, I have met too many miserable people who have pursued paths and jobs that they don't like. They live for the weekends and their next vacation. It's painful and heartbreaking to see. Be courageous and make the change if need be.

"It is never too late to make a change and become who you want to be."

37

The Only Way is College?

According to a 2016 study by the National Center for Education Statistics, 70% of high school students are now going on to college — that's every 7 students in 10. Turn on the TV or radio and you will hear people talking about college being the only option for high schoolers who want to be successful.

Well I am here to tell you that there are plenty of other options available to you. Do not feel pressured into thinking that you need to go to college in order to be successful. This is simply not true.

I am not here saying that nobody needs to go to college. Far from it. If you are planning on pursuing careers within Law, Medicine, Science, Technology, Engineering or Mathematics, then college is certainly the right option for you. These fields need a 4-year degree in order for you to be trained and qualified. **However, more than 25% of jobs nowadays do not need a college degree (Bureau of Labor Statistics).**

We all learn in different ways. Some of us thrive in a classroom, academic-centric environment, while others find they learn best when learning on the job. No one way is better than the other. People who go to college certainly aren't smarter than those that don't. You have other options to explore. College is a viable option, no question, but it simply isn't for everyone.

The National Student Clearinghouse study (2010) highlights that only 58.4% of college students will leave with a diploma — the rest

will dropout; many with high-levels of debt. Do your homework before becoming a statistic and make sure that college is the right decision for you. Don't just follow the crowd.

"There are different types of smart. Everybody has the opportunity to display their smartness differently."

Deciding your next steps after High School is a big decision. There is no doubt about it. I don't want to sway your thoughts either way. Moreover, I want to let you know that you do have options available to you, and I want to give you some ideas to think about:

- **Do your homework.** Not all jobs require a 4-year bachelor's degree. There are many jobs that only require a 2-year associate degree. If the field you want to get in doesn't require a 4-year degree then there is no need to get one. Check out the Bureau for Labor Statistics website and see their Employment Projections for more detailed information (www.bls.gov/emp/ep table 107.htm)

- **Debt & Scholarships.** The average 4-year college student leaves with $37,000 in loan debts (The Economist 2014 study). If you do choose to go to college, are there scholarships you can get to help keep costs down? Spend some time researching options. Can you work while studying to offset some of the cost? There is lots of information online where you can find out about college scholarships and awards. Try www.collegescholarships. org as a place to start.

- **Community College.** Attending a local community college provides you with the opportunity to earn your associate degree without the high costs of a 4-year course. This option allows you to gently make the transition into college life rather than committing to a 4-year program straight away. In most cases you can stay at home and save on accommodation costs. After 2 years you have the option of transferring to a 4-year school and completing your bachelor's degree, or you can move right into your chosen career if it only requires an associate degree.

- **Apprenticeships.** The apprenticeship pathway is far more common in European countries, especially Germany and the UK than in the United States. The US is slowly moving towards offering more apprentice options, however. Basically, apprenticeships provide an opportunity to learn and earn at the same time. You will acquire job specific skills and training relevant to the industry you're in.

- **Year Out.** Taking some time out after High School allows you to stop and gather your thoughts. If you spend time thinking about what you are going to do during the time you take off, then it can be extremely beneficial. You might use this time to travel, visit new places, meet new people and broaden your horizons. You might want to utilize your time to gain some work experience within a particular industry and earn some money at the same time. Whatever you choose to do during a year out — as long as you don't just see it as an opportunity to play video games — it can really help you in working out what it is that you want to do. You'll be even more prepared to go out and start maximizing your potential.

- **Entrepreneurship.** If you have a business idea, then perhaps you might want to pursue that. I'd recommend finding a support network or a mentor who can help you make the right decisions here. There are lots of grants and scholarships out there for the right idea. Building a business is not for everyone; however, don't let the fact that you are young deter you. If you seek out wise counsel and advice it can be a viable option. Remember, have an open mind and don't just follow the crowd.

"Think **differently** than everyone else. Do your **homework** before making huge life decisions."

38

Surf the Waves of Life

If you didn't get the memo or haven't worked it out for yourself yet, I am sorry to be the one to break the news to you: life has ups and downs.

Sometimes you'll feel like you're riding the crest of a wave all the way to the shoreline, whereas other times you might feel like you're being dragged under the water along the ocean floor. These is called LIFE. There is nothing we can to avoid or prevent whatever life throws at us, we can only prepare ourselves to react the best we can.

Having studied successful people and watched how they handle the waves of life, I've realized that they look to adapt to whatever life deals them. Where they can, they are proactive and press on towards being the best they can be regardless of circumstances; however, when life throws them a curveball, they don't get too hysterical, they don't have a tantrum, and they certainly don't complain that life isn't fair. No – they have already done the mental preparation in advance for the times when the waves will come crashing over their heads (<u>when</u>, not <u>if</u>). They are prepared for the tough times, the bad news, the setbacks, the failures, perhaps the loss of a friend or family member. They know that even though life is hard in that moment, it will not always be so. Just like a storm always passes, they hold onto the knowledge that things will get better as long as they hang in. They allow themselves to be disappointed. They give themselves permission to cry and space to grieve, but they don't give up.

"Life has ups and downs. Learn how to handle whatever comes your way. Keep learning. Keep growing. Just don't give up."

But, there are many times in life when everything seems to be going right for us! When this is the case just enjoy it! At the same time, don't let yourself get too carried away. Savor the season you're in but don't get so excited that you lose your focus and begin to feel invincible. This doesn't mean you should be a professional pessimist. Just be wise, and know that another one of life's challenges might be on its way.

One of the best ways to deal with life's up and downs is controlling your mindset. Successful people enjoy the good times and see the challenging times as an opportunity to grow. Life's storms can help us to develop mental toughness, perseverance, grit, determination, gratitude and humility. Maximizing your potential is a journey where we learn on the way, not a one-stop destination. Enjoy the ride!

"Quit trying to stop the waves, it is more fun to learn how to surf."

39

Social Media

Everywhere you go people are updating the world on their lives, posing for selfies and giving their opinions online. Social media is fantastic! It keeps us all connected and the makes the world so much smaller.

Warning

A word of wisdom: please know that whatever you put online can be seen by anyone and everyone. Be smart about what you're putting out there. By all means, use Social Media, but think twice before posting inappropriate photos or posting offensive comments.

Why should you care? After all, you're a free spirit and nobody can hold you back. Well, firstly, you should know that almost all employers research candidates before interviews and especially before offering a job. Nowadays you don't need to hire a private investigator to get the lowdown on someone. No, it's far easier than that. All it takes is simply putting your name into google and pressing enter or searching around on the major social media sites. Even if you're confident that you have the most secure privacy settings possible something always slips out.

Legal laws are now in place whereby someone who has posted something inappropriate or made offensive comments online can be tracked down and prosecuted. For some reason, some people feel that just because they are hidden behind a keyboard, they can say what they want. Well you can't. And if you do and those comments are found to be unlawful, then you can expect to be prosecuted. Then you're chances of getting a job in the future will have been reduced massively. Again, please be smart.

Don't ruin your future by putting something stupid online. Think before you post. Does what you are typing really reflect who you are? Is it kind? Be respectful to other people even if you do not agree with them. Often people type without thinking. Don't upload anything you wouldn't want the world to see. Be smarter than that.

"Think twice before pressing enter on **anything** you post on Social Media. It can't be taken back or undone."

<u>Highlights & Lowlights</u>

Again, social media is a great tool for keeping up with friends and their lives, no matter where they are in the world. Yet, with social media you need to be mindful of falling into the trap of distorted reality.

Remember that people tend to post photos or updates of the good things in their lives. Social Media is a highlight reel. You don't often see people posting photos to tell everyone they are having a bad day or week. No; social media tends to only show us the good stuff in someone's life — which isn't a bad thing at all. Just keep in mind that it is not reality.

It's like models in fashion magazines who have been airbrushed to have a flawless complexion or a six-pack. Few people post about the hard stuff they are dealing with or the setback they are currently dealing with. Just be aware of this and don't fall into the trap of comparing your life to everyone else's through the lens of social media. It's a false reflection of life. If you do find yourself watching other people through social media and measuring your own life against it, then you're only going to disappoint yourself.

Enjoy social media. Utilize all the great and positive stuff that comes from it, but watch what you put out there and don't use social media as a barometer against which to compare your own life.

40

Curiosity

Our world is full of amazing places, people, and ideas. There is so much to discover that no one will ever know everything. So, I want to encourage you to be curious. Be interested in new things, places, and ideas. Ask questions, read, and learn. Try new foods and talk to new people. Don't stick only to what you know because that's where you are comfortable. Go after life with an appetite for discovery. I promise you won't be disappointed. Be childlike in your approach to life. Being curious means that you'll never be bored. You will always have something to get excited about.

Read

Through reading books, you can visit new places, meet amazing people, learn from history, and gain wisdom from some of the world's greatest minds. Being a reader broadens your horizons and can teach you many new things. It will help you arrive at your own opinions and perspectives, reducing your need to simply accept things the way they are. For me, the most exciting thing about reading is knowing that at any moment you can read something that can transform your thoughts and change your life forever!

Have you ever heard a toddler when they are going through their curious stage of asking "Why?" all the time? They question everything! They want to learn, and they want answers. Too many people simply accept things for what they are and don't stop asking any questions when they get older. Or if they do ask questions, they don't go deep enough in their questioning to get the information that is really going to help them. The quality of your life is determined by the questions you ask.

Join your local library and have access to the latest books without spending a penny. Find out about the history of the town or city where you live. Learn about your neighborhood's past. Ask your friends about their backgrounds, their family's heritage, and other interesting things about them. Learning and asking questions bring everything to life and opens up new doors to explore.

"Be **curious** about the world. Read. Ask questions. Open new doors and watch exciting **pathways** begin to appear."

41

Enjoy the Moment

While it's important to have goals and a plan for life, sometimes we just need to sit back and enjoy the moment. As humans we can get caught up in looking to move forward and make progress, and there is nothing wrong in this. In fact, you should have goals and a plan for your life. However, if we are always focused on pressing on and achieving something, we will miss the life that is going on around us.

Once you've got your goals and plans in place, you should be looking to enjoy the moment — enjoy life. If we are too transfixed on getting to the next destination, life can pass us by. We need time to relax and just let go. Rather than worrying about the next thing on our list, we need to accept that we can't control everything. Life is here to be lived and enjoyed.

"Take time to really savor life. Take in the view. Breathe the air. Don't be too busy and miss life."

Don't waste a moment wishing you were older, or more experienced, or had more money, or lived somewhere else. Enjoy where you are at this very moment. Cherish the people in your world. Spend time with them. Invest time into relationships. Enjoy where you live. As long as you have goals and a plan for your life you can relax and know that you are moving forward.

I would suggest taking one day a week to totally switch off from school and work. Dedicate a day to relax and do whatever makes you happy. Maybe it's watching a movie, going for a walk/run, biking, writing, reading, hanging out with friends — whatever it may be. You'll find that by doing this you'll feel much more energized and refreshed. Being too engrossed and tied up in everything isn't healthy. You need time to step back, have fun and recharge your batteries. Getting into the habit of setting one day aside each week will set you up for your later life when things only get more challenging and demanding.

At the same time, you need to understand that, despite having the best laid plans for your life, things don't always work out the way you expected them to. This is ok. Life has a funny way of working out, more often than not in a far better way than what we had originally envisaged.

"So, go ahead make plans for your life. Set goals. But don't forget to look around once in a while. Enjoy the moment and enjoy the journey."

Tips to switch off and relax:

1. Take a day to do something you enjoy

2. Turn off your phone

3. Take a break from social media

4. Get outside for a walk, run or bike ride

5. Meet up with friends

6. Watch a movie

7. Read a book

8. Laugh

These are just suggestions. If there is anything else you like to do to unwind, relax and switch off then go for it!

42

Hang Out with Yourself

Having friends and people you can experience life with is great. At the same time, it's important for you to get comfortable spending time alone. I'm not talking all the time, or even most of the time, just sometimes. Hanging out with yourself allows you to get know who you really are; it gives you the opportunity to learn to be comfortable and understand a bit more about yourself. It gives you time to figure out your tastes, your likes and dislikes, and, most importantly, your uniqueness.

If you constantly spend time with friends, sometimes you can find yourself beginning to wear a mask that hides the real you. It might be the places you go together, the conversations you have, the music you listen to; whatever it is, all of us are constantly being influenced both positively and negatively by the people we associate with most.

Now and again, take a timeout and spend some time alone. This could be going for a walk, reading a book, watching a movie, or simply sitting and watching the world go by. The most important thing is that you are getting to know yourself, not just allowing yourself to be carried along by the waves of life.

We are all unique in our perspectives, quirks, tastes, interests, and desires. In fact, you'll even find that all these change and evolve as you get older. Not learning who they really are is the reason why so many people end up having midlife crises; they suddenly realize in their 40s or 50s that they have drifted to a place in life they don't want to be.

Take some time to listen to your inner voice and to get to know yourself. Having loyal and faithful friends is a must for your life, but ensure you make your best friend yourself.

"Get to know yourself and become comfortable just being you. You are amazing!"

43

Encourage Others

We are all on this journey called life together. While it is important to be competitive and want to do your best in all things, winning should not be at all costs, or at the expense of others. Encourage other people to maximize their own potential that's inside of them and to chase their dreams.

Build your reputation for being an encourager and for championing your friends. Celebrate other people's successes, knowing that if they achieved something great, so can you. Instead of getting jealous or bitter, use their progress and success to motivate yourself to keep on pushing forwards. This way everybody wins.

"Leave people feeling more **inspired** having been in your presence."

If you were to do a survey of the 5 people who you spend most time with, what would they say about you? Would they say you are a positive, life-giving individual, or would they say you leave them feeling drained, tired, and borderline depressed?

Hopefully your friends will describe you as a life-giver, as someone who makes them feel refreshed having spent time in your presence. However, it may be that they, and even yourself, might describe you as a "glass half-empty" type of person, or a little negative. The good news is that you can change. Make sure that you are the type of person you would want to hang out with and the type of friend who brings life to situations. There is nothing worse than being with someone who is constantly negative and thinking the worst. These types of people are tough to be around. They think of every possible problem and every possible worst-case scenario. It's tiring and draining to be around them.

"Would your friends describe you as a life-giver and an inspiration?"

Be the type of person that when your name flashes up on your friends' phone, they want to pick up (instead of them dreading your negativity and heaviness). Aim to be uplifting and excited about life and the lives of your friends. Excitement and enthusiasm are infectious. Strive to be a person who changes the atmosphere in a positive way.

Not only will your friends thank you for being such a positive influence in their lives, you'll begin to see that your friends want to spend more time with you. Your friendships will flourish and go to whole new levels. Now don't get me wrong, there is a time and place for honesty and reality if your friends need to hear it — but there's a way to position and deliver these in a way that can still be constructive.

You cannot begin to imagine how much your life will transform by letting positivity and enthusiasm become your hallmarks.

"Let your words and actions inspire other to never give up. Breathe life into their dreams."

44

Life is Your Own Movie

Forgot Hollywood, the greatest movie or show should be your life. You are the star actor, the lead role. Too many people spend their time watching other people's lives, either on screen or in person, and comparing it to their own. Instead, I want to encourage you to focus on directing the movie of your own life.

To be clear: being the lead role is not about the fame or simply being the star of the show, it is all about life being an adventure. It is about your life being so full with experiences and life that you don't need to live vicariously through other people.

Look to explore. Don't settle for ordinary. Do new things, meet new people, learn new facts and go to new places. Be curious. Be brave. This is your one and only life. Get out and pursue the life you want. Know that things might not always work out the way you want them to, but that's ok. The critical thing is to bring your best each day. Make the most of your unique gifts, skills, talent, and personality. Take risks and don't just stay in the shallow waters. Step out into the deep, get out your comfort zone, and chase after your dreams.

People on their deathbeds can't be heard saying they wished they'd played it safer, or followed someone else's plan for their life; no, they say how they wished they had stayed true to themselves, followed their passions and dreams, taken risks and maximized their life.

Life is your own movie. Don't let it slip by while you are watching someone else's. Be brave, be courageous and then the entertainment will follow.

"You are the star of your own movie. Own it. Don't settle for being an extra."

Humble Pie

What's the main ingredient of a humble pie? It's a big measure of humility.

Humility is another one of the keys that unlocks the door to success. The definition of Being humble is not thinking too much of yourself or considering yourself better than anyone else; it's all about being grateful for the God-given gifts and talents you were born with. Humility is acknowledging everyone who has supported you, encouraged you, and helped you in your life.

To be humble is to be courageous enough to say sorry when you mess up or do something stupid. It's saying you don't know and asking for help when you need it, instead of being too prideful to admit you cannot do something alone. Humility is being gracious in both victory and defeat. Sometimes you win, sometimes you lose, sometimes life doesn't work out the way you might have wanted it. Remember to appreciate every opportunity that life brings you.

You see, some people will tell you that if you put your hand up to say you are struggling or need a helping hand, then you are weak. However, the truth is that the more humility you possess the greater you will become. Once you grasp this truth and live from this place of knowledge, you will see your life transform before you.

So drop the act that you have all the answers. Quickly accept that there will always be greater and lesser persons than yourself, those that know more and those that know less than you. There will always be persons who are more naturally talented than you in an area, and those who are less naturally talented than you. Seek wisdom from the ones more knowledgeable than yourself, and offer wisdom to those who do not have as much experience as you. If you can make friends with humility and walk with it all your life, regardless of where life takes you, you will have been successful.

"We are all **different**. Say thank you. Help people. Be competitive but **remember** life isn't a **competition**."

46

Life is an Adventure Waiting for You

Whether or not you believe that life is an adventure will determine if your life is an adventure or not. In other words, if you want your life to be an adventure, you must see it as one. You must seek out adventure. If you simply see life as being mundane and predictable, then guess what? That's exactly the type of life you're going to experience. But, if you see life as one big journey where you are discovering new things, new ideas, new people and places, that is the type of life you're going to have.

You get to choose how you want to approach your life and live it out. If you don't see life as an adventure, then that's ok. There is no right or wrong way to view life. Personally, I would much rather live a life full of adventure and excitement than one that is boring, slow, and monotonous. If you prefer playing it safe, not speaking to new people, going to new places, or trying new things, that's ok. Again, there is no right or wrong answer here.

You don't have to travel to the other side of the earth or jump out of a plane for your life to be adventurous. Not at all. Living an adventurous life is all about your mindset and how you approach every day. If you treat each day with anticipation of what you might learn, who you might meet, or what might happen to you, then you don't even need to leave your hometown — your life with be so filled with awe and amazement that you will certainly experience adventures. Think about young babies and how everything is new and exciting to them — if you have the right mindset this is the type of life you can live: one full of discovery and wonder. Again, the choice is yours. Adventure or no adventure, that is the question.

"Never stop exploring and never stop learning."

47

Volunteer

Those that volunteer know that what you receive from it far outweighs what you put into it. They know that it is life-transforming to put other people first and take your eyes off yourself every so often. As humans, we are designed to help each other. Those that look to help others quickly realize that there it is much more fun to give than to receive. Instead of not having the time to serve, they know they don't have the time not to serve others.

When you start to give back to your community, something special happens. You begin to understand that everything is not all about you. You start to appreciate other people, and you take your eyes off yourself. Through serving, you learn to be grateful for all you have, and grasp that any challenges you are facing aren't as bad as you first thought.

Volunteering should be something you enjoy. Even if you can only commit to 1 hour per month, I encourage you to do it. Not only will you have fun, you will meet other like-minded people — Remember: you become who you spend the most time with.

Here are some volunteering ideas to get you started:

i.   Mentoring younger students

ii. Cleaning local parks

iii. Visit with elderly people

iv. Help out with disabled people

v.   Local sports club

vi. Help a neighbor with their groceries or clean their yard

vii. You can find lots of opportunities by searching online. Whatever you choose to do, just get out there and do it!

"Take your eyes off yourself and realize life is not all about you after all."

Focus

We live in a world of constant distractions. Someone or something is always competing for your attention, making it very hard to stay focused. Having the skill to concentrate on one task at one time is a dying art form. However, those who can grasp the power of focus will be able to achieve far more than everyone else.

Silence your cellphone when you are looking to concentrate, and tell your family that you need some time alone. You will surprise yourself when you realize how much more you can get done when you're able to focus on one thing at a time.

Don't believe the lie that you can do more than one task at a time. Sure, you can multitask, but it is always at the expense of something. You cannot ask your brain to compute more than one thing at a time and expect it to do everything optimally.

Dr Caroline Leaf is a world famous cognitive neuroscientist who for many years has studied how the brain operates. In her book, Switch On Your Brain (2007) she proves the idea that the ability to multitask is not something to boast about. Dr Leaf explains that our brains cannot do more than one task at a time. Her research shows that multitasking causes neurochemical chaos in our brain, which, in turn, causes literal brain damage! Learning to focus on one task at a time is the skill that will best set you up for success.

Also, know that focus and concentration are skills that can be developed and trained. Don't believe that only some people cannot get distracted. Some people definitely find it easier than others to stay on task, but everyone has the potential to improve their focus.

Tip: Start by trying to focus on one thing for 30 minutes, then gradually build up to an hour then give yourself a break.

"Don't let the barrier to maximizing your potential be the inability to focus."

49

Never Give Up

Life will have up and downs, good times and challenging times. If you haven't experienced them already, you are going to have moments in your life where you want to give in and quit. Hang on in there, know that these times are going to come, and they will always pass. If you want to give up, I want to encourage you to keep pushing forward, and sooner or later you will see some light at the end of the tunnel.

Be Consistent

Being successful and maximizing your potential is a full-time job. This means you need to keep pushing yourself and improving. If you think you can pick and choose when you're going to be the best you can be, you'd better prepare yourself for disappointment. You might see some progress, but you'll soon start to fall backwards. Instead, be consistent. Be intentional. Be focused. Your future self will thank you.

"Never quit. Keep your head up and press on. Don't complain it is too hard, instead find a solution. Keep on fighting every day."

50

Arm Yourself with a Positive Vocabulary

Whether you believe it or not, your words have power. The vocabulary you use it what your ears hear and then feed to your brain. Choose your words wisely.

Words can encourage or discourage, heal or hurt. They can cause destruction, or they can bring life. Always aim to use words that are positive, uplifting and affirming, both to yourself and to other people.

As you begin to start being intentional about your words, you will see your whole perspective start to change. What previously seemed impossible will be filled with hope. With the right vocabulary you can literally speak your bright future into existence!

Start breathing life into your future today. What have you got to lose?

"Your words have power. They can bring life or death. Make sure you are someone who speaks hope into your future and the future of others."

51

Forgive Quickly

One thing that will sidetrack you from becoming all you can be is unforgiveness. Whether it's against a family member, friend, or neighbor, and for whatever reason, you need to deal with it. Carrying around unforgiveness creates bitterness, which is hard work. It's heavy and will slow you down.

"If you can't **forgive** others, then don't expect them to forgive you when you need it. Trust me, you **will** need it."

Forgive quickly and forgive often. We are humans, we do and say stupid things at times. Unforgiveness hurts you more than it hurts the other person. Plus, you never know when you might need some forgiveness yourself.

52

Laugh at Yourself

If you are committed to maximizing your potential, you're going to need to get serious; but not too serious! Along the pathway to success there are going to be times when things don't work out the way you wanted; you mess up, make silly mistakes, or do something and you have no idea why you did it. These are the times when, rather than beating yourself up, you need to laugh!

Go easy on yourself. Life can get heavy and intense if you take yourself too seriously all the time. Lighten up. Enjoy the journey. Nobody's perfect and there isn't an exact formula you should be following. Laugh at yourself and then go again.

If a friend is feeling down, cheer them up by making them laugh. Laughing changes everything and reminds us nothing is that bad after all!

"Nothing is too serious or important that you can't laugh about it. If you aren't laughing, you aren't living. Laugh, smile, have fun. Repeat."

53

Weird is Cool

We are all made differently. Every one of us is unique in our own way. So why are so many people in a hurry to be like everyone else?

If you think differently to everyone else, so what? You might dress differently than other people, so what? You might see the world in a way unlike everyone else, and so what? You are you. You've been made this way for a reason. These are your gifts to bring to the world. Don't be in a rush to hide, or water down who you are. Be brave. Be different.

Conforming and blending in with the crowd is the safe option. It is easy. Staying true to who you are and standing strong when you know you are different takes courage. Being the odd one out can be uncomfortable. It can be lonely. People might look at you strangely, or even say mean things to you. They might call you weird. It can be tough staying true to who you are — but even if that's means you're different, that's cool.

Weird is about being different and being ok with it, rather than worrying what others might think. Eventually you will realize people didn't care too much anyway.

Maximizing your potential is about staying true to who you are. In fact, you can't fulfill your potential if you aren't being you. It is impossible. Embrace who you are and celebrate the fact there is only one of you.

"Think different. Be **strange**. Don't conform. You do you. Weird is the new **cool**."

54

Create, Don't Just Consume

Whatever you want to do, buy, read, watch or eat, in the modern world you are spoiled with choices. You have unlimited options in front of you. Having so many possibilities isn't a bad thing, but it can lead to you only being a consumer. In other words, you just take, take, take, without putting anything back. This type of mindset usually goes hand-in-hand with complaining. You become so used to having everything you need at your fingertips that you stop thinking. You just consume. And all the creativity that is within you just dries up.

I challenge you to be creative. Don't just consume. If you see a problem in the world, can you try to solve it instead of complaining? Can you think differently than the crowd? It can be anything. For example, it could be a business solution like an app or website, or something in your school, or a community need. Perhaps you like playing board games: can you start a group at school that meets to play together? Maybe you want to start helping mentor younger children in your neighborhood. Or maybe you start a blog on a subject you enjoy.

"Think **differently**. Don't wait and expect the world to serve you. Go and **create** your own solutions."

It doesn't matter what you choose to do, the main thing is that you are looking at the world differently. You begin to see things with a solution mindset. Instead of just waiting for somebody else to create something you can consume or attend, you become a creator.

Once you become a creator, everything changes. Your future is limitless. If you don't like something, you can to do something about it. Wish something was different? Build something better. As a creator, you start to take control of your future, instead of just being a passenger.

The best way to start on your way to becoming a creator is to think about something in your life that you wish was better, or something you wished existed. Don't limit your thinking. Think big and don't worry about how you will do it. The biggest challenge is having the idea in the first place. Bringing ideas to life is easier than having the creative ideas in the first place. People will want to help you once you have a great idea.

Here are some starting questions that will help you as you shift towards a creator mindset:

1. Describe something or someplace (physical or online) that either frustrates you, or you wish existed.

2. Explain why it frustrates you, or why you wish it existed.

3. Is there anything similar that currently exists?

4. What skills do you think you would need to start creating this?

5. What doubts or fears do you have about bringing this to life?

6. Who can you share this idea with you will help you take the next step?

So, go out and create. Think differently. Use your unique thoughts and perspectives to make the word better. Solve problems for people. By doing so you will learn a tremendous amount (remember there is no failure only feedback), your mindset will change for ever, and you will be well on your way to maximizing your potential. Go and create.

55

Now It's Your Turn

Well done for reaching the end of the book! I have some good news and bad news. Bad news: reading is the easy part. Anyone can read a book on maximizing their potential; but, unless you take action and start to put some of these pieces of advice into practice, nothing will change. Good news: You already have what it takes to maximize your potential. You can start today. It isn't easy, but anybody can do it. It is up to you how much you want it.

Lastly, maximizing your potential is not an exact formula. The advice in this book is not everything you need to know, it is merely a starter. Becoming the best you can be and living a big life is a journey. Should you choose to embark upon it, you will be forever learning new ideas and wisdom. My hope is that you start on your own journey, and you get serious about living your one life to the maximum. Have no regrets, be yourself and don't compare yourself to others, take action, treat people as you'd like to be treated, dream big, and laugh a lot. Most importantly, enjoy the ride!

"Live your life with action. Don't wait for something to change. Take ownership and make sure you don't have any regrets."

Let's Continue the Journey Together...

Connect with us at www.Growing-Potential.com

If you are a teenager, we would love to help you as you move towards maximizing your potential.

Let us know the action steps you have taken since reading the book, or what your goals and dreams are. We would love to hear from you!

Email us - info@growing-potential.com

Join our Facebook community, and connect with other people who are committed to being their best.

www.growing-potential.com

58610557R00075

Made in the USA
Middletown, DE
07 August 2019